Star-Studded
Quilts

Star-Studded Quilts

SAMPLER BLOCKS TO MIX AND MATCH

ROXANNE CARTER

Acknowledgments

I would like to thank all my students for their help and encouragement while I was writing this book. Their comments and enthusiasm kept me going. My students repeatedly tell me how much fun they have in class and how they love their sampler quilts when they're finished. Thanks to you all. I would also like to thank my husband, Rob, for all his help and understanding while I was working on the computer to write this book.

Star-Studded Quilts: Sampler Blocks to Mix and Match
© 2004 by Roxanne Carter

That Patchwork Place® is an imprint of Martingale & Company®.

Martingale & Company
20205 144th Avenue NE
Woodinville, WA 98072-8478 USA
www.martingale-pub.com

Printed in China
09 08 07 06 05 04   8 7 6 5 4 3 2 1

Library of Congress Cataloging-in-Publication Data
Carter, Roxanne.
    Star-studded quilts: sampler blocks to mix and match / Roxanne Carter.
        p. cm.
Includes bibliographical references and index.
    ISBN 1-56477-538-0
    1. Patchwork—Patterns. 2. Quilting—Patterns.
    3. Star quilts. I. Title.
    TT835.C3914 2004
    746.46—dc22
                                                    2003027313

Credits

President ★ *Nancy J. Martin*
CEO ★ *Daniel J. Martin*
Publisher ★ *Jane Hamada*
Editorial Director ★ *Mary V. Green*
Managing Editor ★ *Tina Cook*
Technical Editor ★ *Ellen Pahl*
Copy Editor ★ *Kathy P. Bradley*
Design Director ★ *Stan Green*
Illustrator ★ *Laurel Strand*
Cover Designer ★ *Stan Green*
Text Designer ★ *Regina Girard*
Photographer ★ *Brent Kane*

Mission Statement

Dedicated to providing quality products and service to inspire creativity.

Contents

6   Introduction

7   Piecing

8   Binding

10   THE BLOCKS

     11   Arrow Crown

     12   Aurora

     14   Carpenter's Wheel

     16   Diamond Star

     17   Dutch Rose

     19   Land of the Midnight Sun

     21   Martha's Star

     22   Next-Door Neighbor

     24   Pieced Stars

     25   Snow Crystals

     27   Star of Magi

     29   Union Square

     31   Whirlwind

     32   Wyoming Valley Star

34   Cutting Chart for Blocks

37   THE QUILTS

     37   Lap-Size Star-Studded Sampler

     41   Queen-Size Star-Studded Sampler

     45   King-Size Star-Studded Sampler

     49   Sweet Pea Sampler

     54   Star Quartet

     58   Trio of Stars Table Runner

     60   Around the Block Tote Bag

63   About the Author

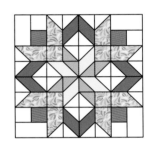

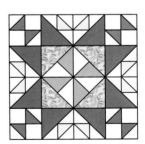

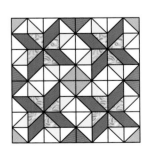

Introduction

I love making sampler quilts, and I wrote this book for all the other quilters out there who share my passion. I have included 14 blocks, along with several projects that use any of those blocks. Since they are all 12" blocks, you can mix and match blocks in any of the quilts. The yardages given for each quilt are sufficient to complete the quilt top, no matter which blocks you choose.

Some of the block designs were in my book *All-Star Sampler* (That Patchwork Place, 1995), but in that book they were made using diamonds. In this book, you can make them with simple squares, rectangles, and triangles. This makes the construction of the blocks much easier, and the results are virtually the same. The cutting and piecing instructions are given in detail for each block. I've also included a handy cutting chart for all 14 blocks beginning on page 34. Use this if you want to cut the pieces for all the blocks at once.

I hope you enjoy the blocks and projects in this book as much as my students and I have. Now, select your quilt, choose your blocks, and have fun!

Piecing

Traditional quilts are my passion, and I delight in finding the easiest way to piece them. I have incorporated rotary cutting into all my quilts and follow that up with sewing methods that will almost guarantee success. Be sure to sew with an accurate ¼" seam allowance, and press each piece after it is sewn.

Folded-Corners Technique

Most of the blocks include the folded-corners technique in their construction. This method makes the cutting and sewing quick and easy; you do not need to cut triangles or sew along bias edges.

1. Place a smaller square on a corner of a larger square or rectangle, right sides together.

2. Draw a diagonal line from corner to corner on the smaller square and sew on the line.

3. Use a rotary cutter and ruler to trim the seam allowance to ¼". Press the seam toward the triangle or follow the pressing arrows in the block instructions.

Another option is to sew the diagonal seam without marking, using the tape method.

1. Lower the needle into the machine and place a ruler next to the needle. Use either masking tape or blue painter's tape to "draw" a line in front of the needle with the tape.

2. Place the square on the corner of the larger square or rectangle and put one corner of the square at the needle and the opposite diagonal

corner on the edge of the tape. Keeping the corner of the square aligned with the edge of the tape, sew the seam. Trim the excess and press.

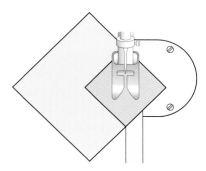

Layered-Squares Technique

To make standard triangle-square units, I use the layered-squares method, which is another method that eliminates cutting triangles and sewing along bias edges. Simply cut two squares, mark a diagonal line, stitch, and cut.

1. Place the two squares right sides together and draw a diagonal line from one corner to the opposite corner.

2. Sew with a ¼" seam allowance on both sides of the drawn line.

Teacher's Tip
If you don't have a ¼" foot on your machine, you may want to mark the sewing lines as well as the cutting line. Draw the sewing lines ¼" from both sides of the first diagonal line.

3. Cut on the drawn line and press the seams toward the darker fabric, or as shown by the arrows in the block diagrams.

Binding

 For a traditional binding, cut strips across the width of the fabric and piece the strips on the bias. The only time you need a bias binding is when you have a quilt with a scalloped or curved edge, such as a Double Wedding Ring.

1. Cut 2½" strips across the width of the fabric. Strips of this width will result in a finished binding width of approximately ⅜" to ½", depending on the thickness of your batting. The directions for each project include the number of strips to cut.

2. Place two strips right sides together with the ends positioned as shown. Sew a diagonal seam from one corner to the opposite corner. Trim the seam to ¼" and press the seam open.

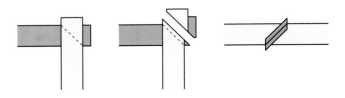

3. Fold the strip in half lengthwise, wrong sides together, and press.

4. Position the strip on the right side of the quilt, aligning it with the edge of the quilt. Leave 6" free and begin sewing in the middle of the side. Use a walking foot and stitch the binding to the quilt with a ¼" seam allowance.

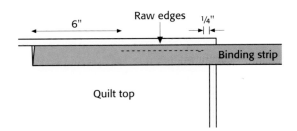

5. When you reach a corner, stop stitching ¼" from the edge, and backstitch. Remove the quilt from the machine and fold the binding

Teacher's Tip

When sewing on binding, use a walking foot or even-feed mechanism if you have one. It helps feed the layers through the machine evenly.

up and away from the quilt, creating a 45° angle as shown.

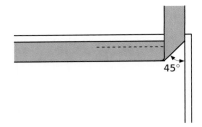

6. Fold the binding down, aligning the raw edges with the next side of the quilt, and begin stitching ¼" from the folded binding edge. Continue stitching around the quilt to within 6" of the starting point.

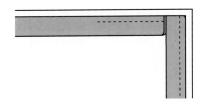

7. Remove the quilt from the machine and fold both strips back so that the folded edges meet about 3" from both lines of the stitching as shown. The binding should lie flat on the quilt. Finger-press to crease the folds. Cut both strips 1¼" from the fold.

8. Open both strips and place the ends at right angles to each other, right sides together. Match the points where the center creases meet the finger-pressed fold. Fold the bulk of the quilt out of your way. Join the strips with a diagonal seam as shown.

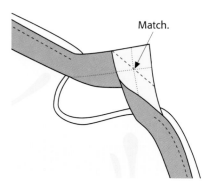

Match.

9. Trim the seam to ¼" and press it open. Fold the joined strips so that the wrong sides are together again. Place the binding flat against the quilt and finish stitching it to the quilt.

10. Trim the layers even with the edge of the quilt. Fold the binding to the back of the quilt and blindstitch it to the back, covering the seam line and mitering the corners.

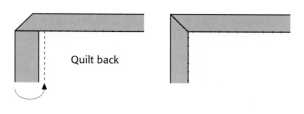

Quilt back

The Blocks

All of the blocks are made from six different fabrics.

- **Main Print.** This is the fabric I choose first. It is usually a multicolor print; I often use it in the border of the quilt, to tie it all together.

- **Dark, Medium, and Light.** These are usually tone-on-tone prints that coordinate with the main print.

- **Strong Accent.** This fabric might coordinate or contrast with the others. It could be a stronger version of one of the other fabrics in the same color, or a color that is opposite one of the others on the color wheel. Again, I often use a tone-on-tone print for this.

- **Background.** I usually choose a white-on-white print or a pale color for the background fabric of my blocks. This allows the other colors to stand out, and highlights the piecing in the blocks to let the stars really shine.

The finished size of each block is 12" x 12". Use them in any of the quilts in the book, or have fun, be creative, and design your own quilt with them.

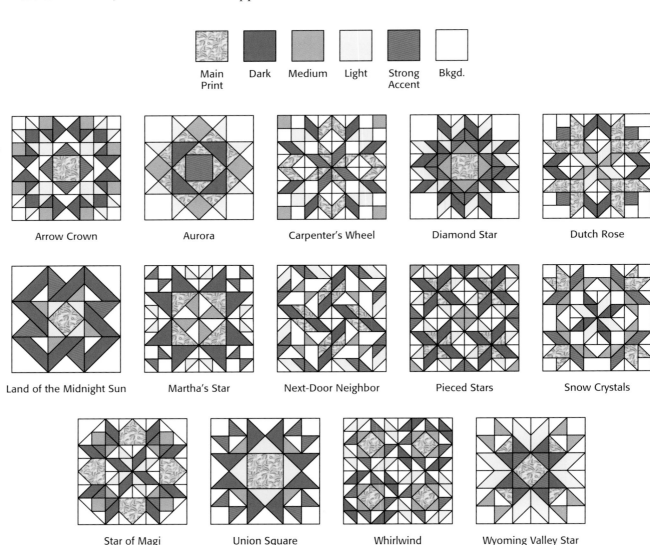

Main Print   Dark   Medium   Light   Strong Accent   Bkgd.

Arrow Crown   Aurora   Carpenter's Wheel   Diamond Star   Dutch Rose

Land of the Midnight Sun   Martha's Star   Next-Door Neighbor   Pieced Stars   Snow Crystals

Star of Magi   Union Square   Whirlwind   Wyoming Valley Star

Arrow Crown

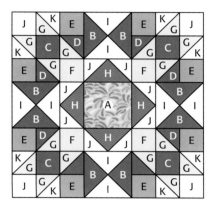

Fabric	Piece	Number and Size to Cut
Main print	A	1 square, 3½" x 3½"
Dark	B	2 squares, 4¼" x 4¼"
	C	4 squares, 2" x 2"
	D	4 squares, 2⅜" x 2⅜"
Medium	E	8 squares, 2" x 2"
Light	F	4 squares, 2" x 2"
	G	8 squares, 2⅜" x 2⅜"
Strong accent	H	4 rectangles, 2" x 3½"
Background	I	2 squares, 4¼" x 4¼"
	J	12 squares, 2" x 2"
	K	4 squares, 2⅜" x 2⅜"

Piecing

1. Place four 2⅜" light squares right sides together with four 2⅜" background squares. Use the "Layered-Squares Technique" (page 7) to make triangle squares. Press the seams toward the light fabric. Make eight triangle squares. Repeat with the remaining 2⅜" light squares right sides together with the 2⅜" dark squares. Make eight triangle squares.

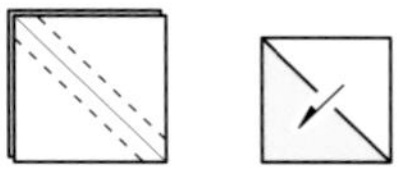

Make 8. 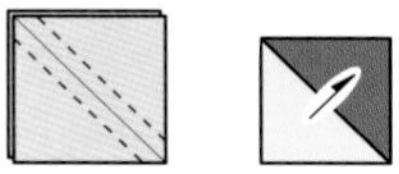   Make 8.

2. Using the 2" light, medium, dark, and background squares and the units from step 1, assemble the block-corner units as shown. Press the seams in the direction of the arrows. Make four.

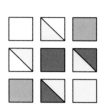 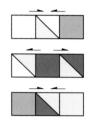

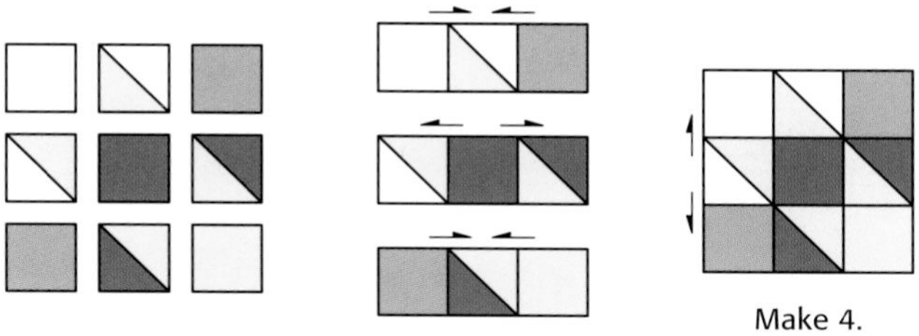

Make 4.

3. Place the two 4¼" dark squares right sides together with the 4¼" background squares. Make four triangle squares using the layered-squares technique. Press the seam toward the dark fabric.

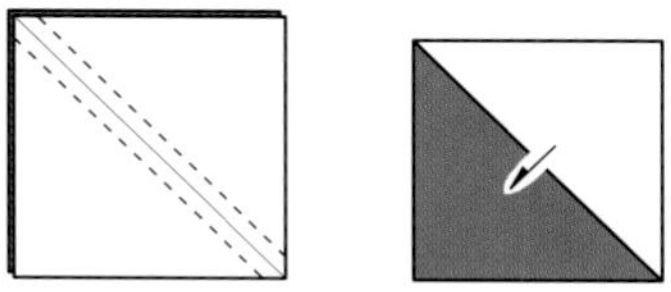

Make 4.

4. Place two of the triangle squares from step 3 right sides together so that the dark triangles are opposite each other. Draw a diagonal line as shown and sew with a ¼" seam allowance on both sides of the line. Cut the squares apart on the line. Make four quarter squares.

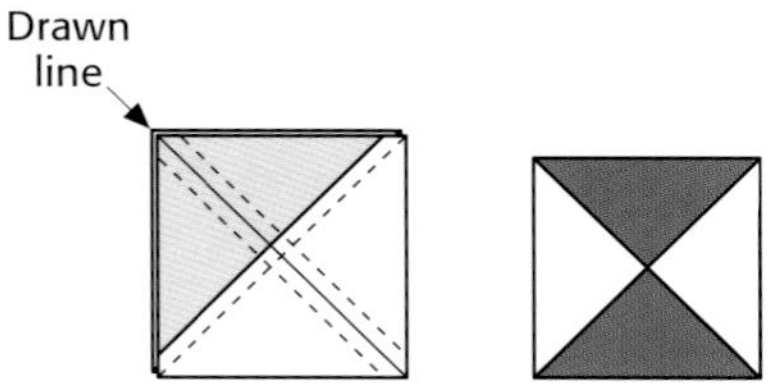

Drawn line

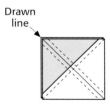

Make 4.

5. Place a 2" background square on one corner of a 2" x 3½" strong-accent rectangle. Use the "Folded-Corners Technique" (page 7) and sew on the drawn line. Trim and press the seam toward the background triangle. Repeat with another 2" background square on the other corner, reversing the angle. Make four.

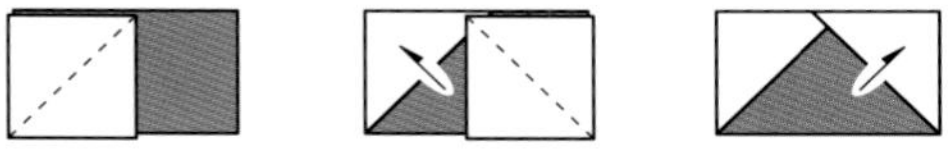

Make 4.

6. Sew the quarter squares from step 4 to the units from step 5, as shown. Press as indicated by the arrow. Make four.

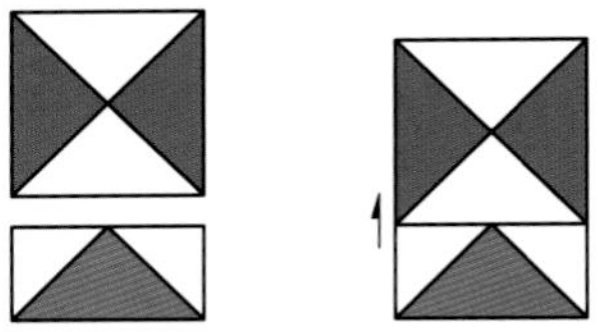

Make 4.

7. Assemble the block, using the 3½" main-print square in the center. Press as indicated by the arrows.

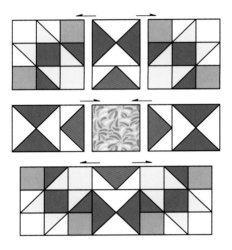

Aurora

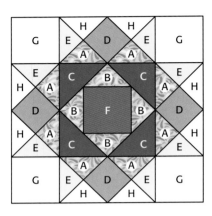

Fabric	Piece	Number and Size to Cut
Main print	A	2 squares, 4¼" x 4¼"
	B	2 squares, 3" x 3", cut once diagonally
Dark	C	2 squares, 3⅞" x 3⅞", cut once diagonally
Medium	D	4 squares, 2⅝" x 2⅝"
Light	E	2 squares, 4¼" x 4¼"
Strong accent	F	1 square, 3½" x 3½"
Background	G	4 squares, 3½" x 3½"
	H	2 squares, 4¼" x 4¼", cut twice diagonally

Piecing

1. Place the 4¼" light and 4¼" main-print squares right sides together. Use the "Layered-Squares Technique" (page 7) to make four triangle squares. Cut them in half once diagonally.

Make 4.

2. Sew two 4¼" background triangles to the sides of a 2⅝" medium square. Press the seams as indicated by the arrows. Make four.

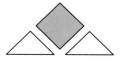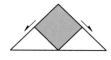

Make 4.

3. Sew the units from step 1 to the units from step 2, as shown. Press the seams as indicated by the arrows. Make four.

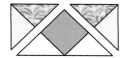

Make 4.

4. Sew two 3" main-print triangles to opposite sides of the 3½" strong-accent square. Press toward the triangles. Sew the remaining main-print triangles to the other two sides. Press.

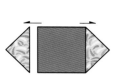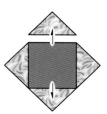

5. Sew two 3⅞" dark triangles to opposite sides of the unit from step 4. Repeat with the remaining dark triangles. Press.

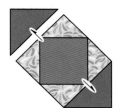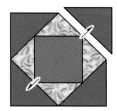

6. Using the 3½" background squares and the units made in the preceding steps, sew the block together as shown. Press the seams as indicated by the arrows.

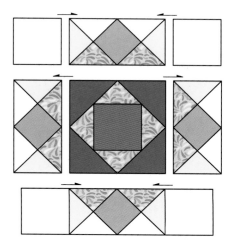

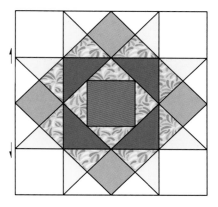

Carpenter's Wheel

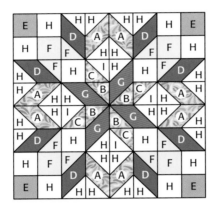

Fabric	Piece	Number and Size to Cut
Main print	A	8 rectangles, 2" x 3½"
	B	4 squares, 2" x 2"
	C	2 squares, 2⅜" x 2⅜"
Dark	D	8 rectangles, 2" x 3½"
Medium	E	4 squares, 2" x 2"
Light	F	12 squares, 2" x 2"
Strong accent	G	4 rectangles, 2" x 3½"
Background	H	40 squares, 2" x 2"
	I	2 squares, 2⅜" x 2⅜"

Piecing

1. Using the "Folded-Corners Technique" (page 7), place a 2" background square on a 2" x 3½" dark rectangle. Sew from corner to corner. Make four in each direction. Press the seams as indicated by the arrows. Repeat with the 2" light squares on the opposite end, keeping the angles the same. Trim and press the seams as indicated by the arrows.

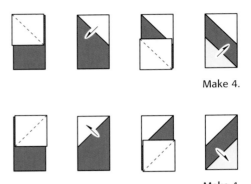

Make 4.

Make 4.

2. Sew two 2" background squares on each of the 2" x 3½" main-print rectangles, again using the folded-corners technique and keeping the angles the same in each. Make four in each direction. Trim and press.

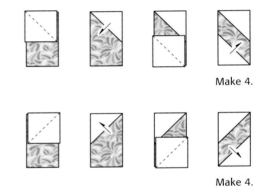

Make 4.

Make 4.

3. Sew the 2" background squares on the 2" x 3½" strong-accent rectangles, using the folded-corners technique. Repeat with the 2" main-print squares on the opposite end, keeping the angles the same. Trim and press.

Make 4.

4. Place the 2⅜" main-print squares and the 2⅜" background squares right sides together and use the "Layered-Squares Technique" (page 7) to make triangle squares. Press the seams toward the main print. Make four triangle squares.

Make 4.

5. Sew the triangle squares to the 2" background squares.

Make 4.

6. Sew the units from step 3 to the triangle-square units from step 5. Press. Make four.

Make 4.

7. Assemble the center star as shown. Press.

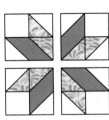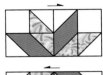

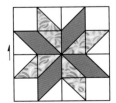

8. Assemble the block side units as shown. Press as indicated by the arrows. Make four.

Make 4.

9. Using the remaining 2" background, medium, and light squares, make the corner four-patch units as shown. Press. Make four.

Make 4.

10. Assemble the block as shown. Press.

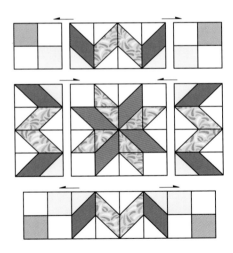

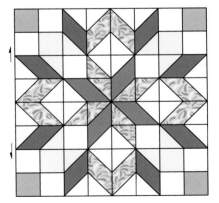

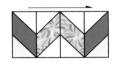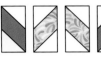

Diamond Star

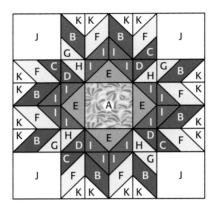

Fabric	Piece	Number and Size to Cut
🖼 Main print	A	1 square, 3½" x 3½"
⬛ Dark	B	8 rectangles, 2" x 3½"
	C	4 squares, 2" x 2"
	D	2 squares, 2⅜" x 2⅜"
▨ Medium	E	4 rectangles, 2" x 3½"
☐ Light	F	8 rectangles, 2" x 3½"
	G	4 squares, 2" x 2"
	H	2 squares, 2⅜" x 2⅜"
▨ Strong accent	I	16 squares, 2" x 2"
☐ Background	J	4 squares, 3½" x 3½"
	K	16 squares, 2" x 2"

Piecing

1. Using the "Folded-Corners Technique" (page 7), place a 2" strong-accent square on one corner of each 2" x 3½" medium rectangle. Sew a diagonal seam, trim, and press. Repeat with the other corner, as shown, to make four.

Make 4.

2. Place a 2⅜" dark and a 2⅜" light square right sides together. Use the "Layered-Squares Technique" (page 7) to sew triangle-square units. Cut the squares apart on the line and press the seams toward the darker fabric. Make four.

Make 4.

3. Using the folded-corners technique, place a 2" background square on one end of each of the 2" x 3½" dark rectangles and sew a diagonal seam. Trim and make eight units. Add a 2" strong-accent square to the opposite corner of four of the units. Add a 2" light square to the opposite corner of the other four units. Keep the angles the same.

Make 4.   Make 4.

4. Repeat with the 2" x 3½" light rectangles and 2" background squares as shown, with the angles reversed. Trim and make eight units. Add a strong-accent square to four of the units. Add a dark square on the opposite corner of the other four units. Keep the angles the same.

Make 4.   Make 4.

5. Sew the units from steps 3 and 4 together as shown, pressing as indicated. Make four.

    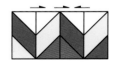

Make 4.

6. Assemble the center of the block as shown, using the 3½" main-print square in the center. Press.

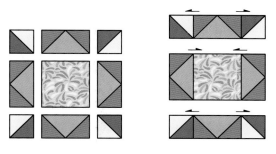

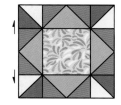

7. Assemble the block, using the units from steps 5 and 6 and the 3½" background squares. Press.

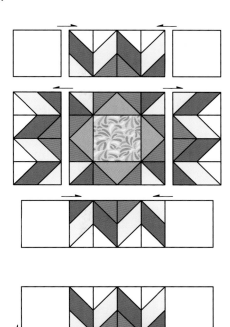

Dutch Rose

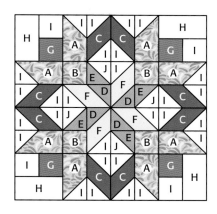

Fabric	Piece	Number and Size to Cut
Main print	A	8 rectangles, 2" x 3½"
	B	4 squares, 2" x 2"
Dark	C	8 rectangles, 2" x 3½"
Medium	D	4 squares, 2" x 2"
	E	2 squares, 2⅜" x 2⅜"
Light	F	4 rectangles, 2" x 3½"
Strong accent	G	4 squares, 2" x 2"
Background	H	4 rectangles, 2" x 3½"
	I	32 squares, 2" x 2"
	J	2 squares, 2⅜" x 2⅜"

Piecing

1. Using the "Folded-Corners Technique" (page 7), place the 2" background squares on the 2" x 3½" dark rectangles and sew from corner to corner. Make four in each direction. Sew another 2" background square on the opposite end, keeping the angles the same. Trim the

excess fabric and press the seams as indicated by the arrows.

Make 4.

Make 4.

2. Sew the 2" background squares on the 2" x 3½" light rectangles. Repeat with the 2" medium squares on the opposite end, keeping the angles the same. Trim and press. Make four.

Make 4.

3. Sew the 2" background squares on one end of the 2" x 3½" main-print rectangles. Trim and press. Make four in each direction.

Make 4.   Make 4.

4. Use the "Layered-Squares Technique" (page 7) to make the triangle-square units. Place the 2⅜" medium squares right sides together with the 2⅜" background squares. Stitch, cut, and press the seam toward the medium fabric. Trim off any dog-ears. Make four triangle-square units.

Make 4.

5. Sew the triangle-square units to the 2" main-print squares. Press the seams toward the main-print squares. Make four.

Make 4.

6. Sew the units from step 2 to the units from step 5. Press the seams in the direction of the arrow. Make four.

Make 4.

7. Assemble the center star as shown, using the units from step 6. Press.

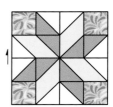

8. Sew the 2" background squares to the 2" strong-accent squares. Press. Make four. Sew a 2" x 3½" background rectangle to each of the units just made. Press.

Make 4.

9. Sew the units from steps 1 and 3 together as shown. Press the seams as indicated by the arrows. Make four.

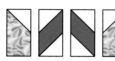

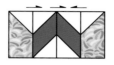

Make 4.

10. Assemble the block as shown. Press.

Land of the Midnight Sun

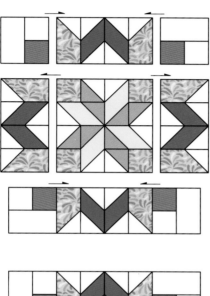

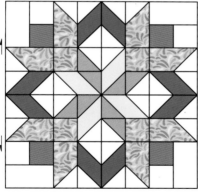

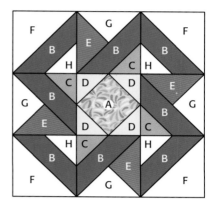

Fabric	Piece	Number and Size to Cut
Main print	A	1 square, 4½" x 4½"
Dark	B	4 squares, 4⅞" x 4⅞", cut once diagonally
Medium	C	4 squares, 2½" x 2½"
Light	D	4 squares, 2½" x 2½"
Strong accent	E	1 square, 5¼" x 5¼", cut twice diagonally
Background	F	2 squares, 4⅞" x 4⅞", cut once diagonally
	G	1 square, 5¼" x 5¼", cut twice diagonally
	H	4 squares, 2½" x 2½"

Piecing

1. Place a 2½" background square on the right-angle corner of each of four 4⅞" dark triangles. Sew from corner to corner and trim the excess fabric to ¼". Press the seams toward the dark fabric. Make four. Repeat with the 2½" medium

squares on the remaining 4⅞" dark triangles. Press. Make four.

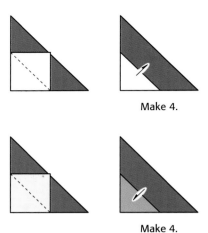

Make 4.

Make 4.

2. Sew a 4⅞" background triangle to the edge of each of the four dark/background units from step 1. Press.

Make 4.

3. Sew the triangles cut from the 5¼" strong-accent and background squares together as shown. Press toward the darker fabric. Make four.

Make 4.

4. Sew the dark/medium units from step 1 to the strong-accent/background units from step 3. Press the seams toward the step 1 units. Make four.

Make 4.

5. Place two 2½" light squares on opposite corners of the 4½" main-print square. Use the "Folded-Corners Technique" (page 7) to sew the squares. Trim, and press the seams toward the light fabric. Repeat with the remaining 2½" light squares on the other corners.

Make 1.

6. Assemble the block in rows as shown. Press as indicated by the arrows.

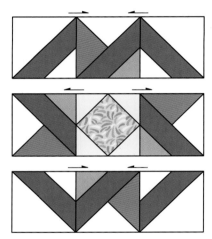

The Blocks

Martha's Star

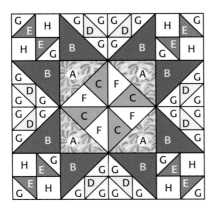

Fabric	Piece	Number and Size to Cut
Main print	A	2 squares, 3⅞" x 3⅞", cut once diagonally
Dark	B	4 squares, 3⅞" x 3⅞", cut once diagonally
Medium	C	2 squares, 3" x 3"
Light	D	4 squares, 2⅜" x 2⅜"
Strong accent	E	4 squares, 2⅜" x 2⅜"
Background	F	2 squares, 3" x 3"
	G	16 squares, 2⅜" x 2⅜"; cut 8 once diagonally
	H	8 squares, 2" x 2"

Piecing

1. Place the 3" medium squares right sides together with the 3" background squares. Use the "Layered-Squares Technique" (page 7) to make four triangle squares. Press the seams toward the medium. Trim off any dog-ears.

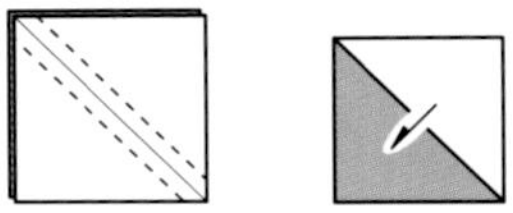

Make 4.

2. Place the 2⅜" strong-accent squares right sides together with four of the 2⅜" background squares to make eight triangle squares. Repeat with the 2⅜" light and 2⅜" background squares to make eight of each combination. Press.

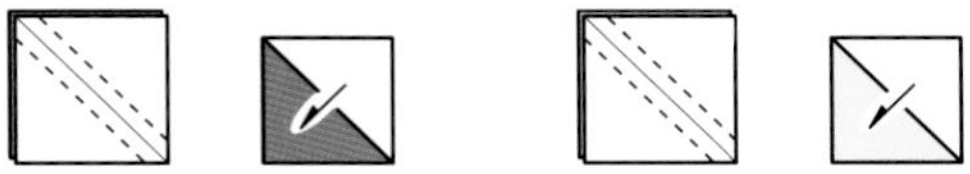

Make 8.   Make 8.

3. Sew the triangle squares from step 1 together to form the center pinwheel. Press as indicated by the arrows.

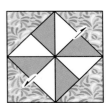

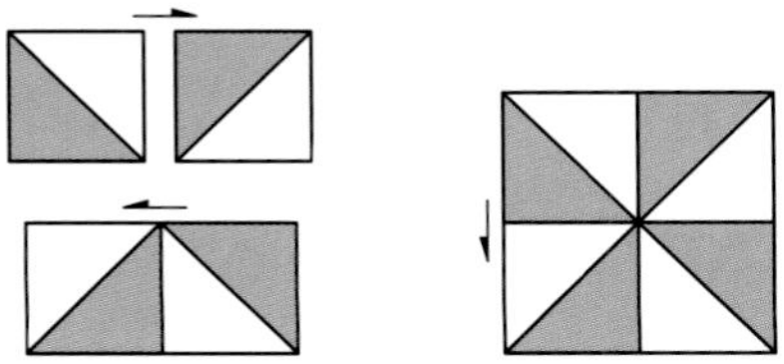

Make 1.

4. Sew two 3⅞" main-print triangles to opposite sides of the center pinwheel. Press. Repeat with the remaining main-print triangles.

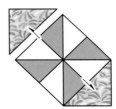

5. Using the 2" background squares and the strong-accent triangle squares, assemble four corner units for the block. Press.

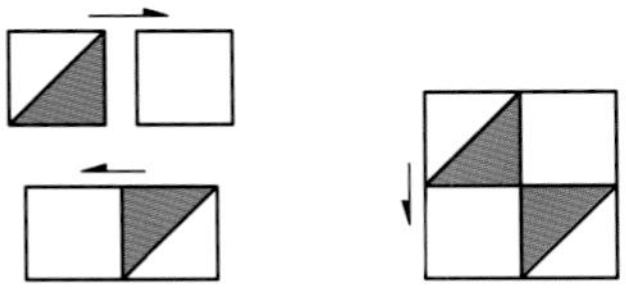

Make 4.

6. Sew two of the 2⅜" background triangles to the sides of the light triangle squares from step 2. Press the seams in the directions of the arrows. Make eight.

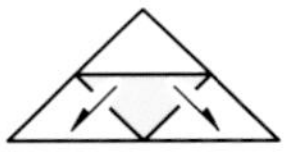

Make 8.

7. Sew the 3⅞" dark triangles to the units from step 6. Press. Make eight.

Make 8.

8. Sew two units from step 7 together as shown. Press. Make four.

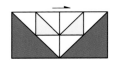

Make 4.

9. Assemble the block as shown. Press in the direction of the arrows.

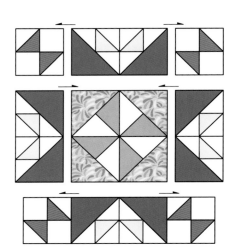

Next-Door Neighbor

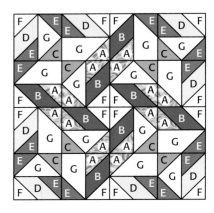

Fabric	Piece	Number and Size to Cut
Main print	A	16 squares, 2" x 2"
Dark	B	8 rectangles, 2" x 3½"
Medium	C	8 squares, 2" x 2"
Light	D	8 rectangles, 2" x 3½"
Strong accent	E	16 squares, 2" x 2"
Background	F	16 squares, 2" x 2"
	G	16 rectangles, 2" x 3½"

Piecing

1. Using the "Folded-Corners Technique" (page 7), place a 2" main-print square on one end of a 2" x 3½" dark rectangle. Sew from corner to corner. Trim, and press the seam toward the main print. Repeat with a 2" background square on the opposite end. Keep the angle the same. Press the seam toward the background. Make eight of these units.

Make 8.

2. Repeat step 1 with a strong-accent square on one corner of a 2" x 3½" light rectangle and a 2" background square on the opposite end. Keep the angle the same. Make eight.

Make 8.

3. Place a 2" main-print square on the corner of a 2" x 3½" background rectangle. Sew from corner to corner, using the opposite angle from that used in steps 1 and 2. Trim, and press the seams toward the main print. Repeat with a 2" strong-accent square. Make eight of each combination.

Make 8.   Make 8.

4. On four of the background/main-print units from step 3, place a 2" medium square on the opposite corner. Sew from corner to corner. Trim, and press the seams toward the medium. Repeat with four of the background/strong-accent units from step 3.

Make 4.

Make 4.

5. Make four of each unit as shown.

Make 4 of each.

6. Sew the units from step 5 together as shown. Make four units.

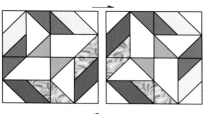

Make 4.

7. Assemble the block as shown. Press.

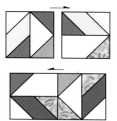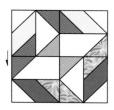

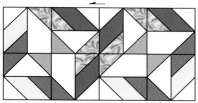

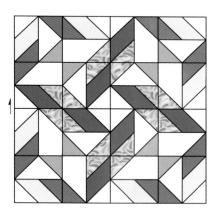

Pieced Stars

Fabric	Piece	Number and Size to Cut
Main print	A	16 squares, 2" x 2"
Dark	B	16 rectangles, 2" x 3½"
Medium	C	4 squares, 2⅜" x 2⅜"
Light	D	8 squares, 2⅜" x 2⅜"
Strong accent	E	4 squares, 2⅜" x 2⅜"
Background	F	16 squares, 2" x 2"
	G	16 squares, 2⅜" x 2⅜"

Piecing

1. Using the "Layered-Squares Technique" (page 7), place the 2⅜" background squares right sides together with the strong-accent, medium, and light squares. Draw the diagonal line on the background squares. Sew with a ¼" seam allowance on both sides of the line. Cut the squares apart on the line and press the seams toward the darker fabric.

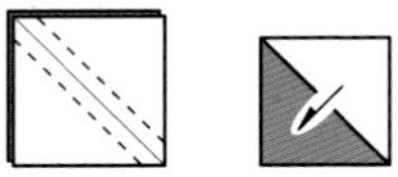

Make 8. 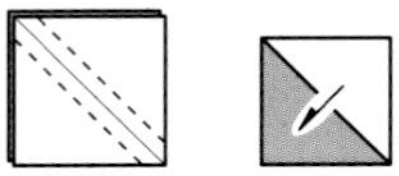   Make 8.

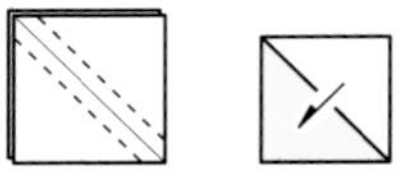

Make 16.

2. Sew the light and medium triangle squares together as shown. Repeat with the strong-accent and light triangle squares. Make eight of each combination.

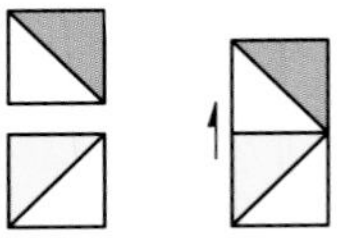

Make 8. 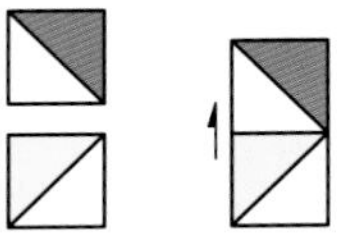   Make 8.

3. Using the "Folded-Corners Technique" (page 7), sew the 2" background squares on one corner of the 2" x 3½" dark rectangles. Repeat with the 2" main-print squares on the other corner. Keep the angle the same. Trim the excess to ¼" and press the seams away from the dark fabric. Make 16.

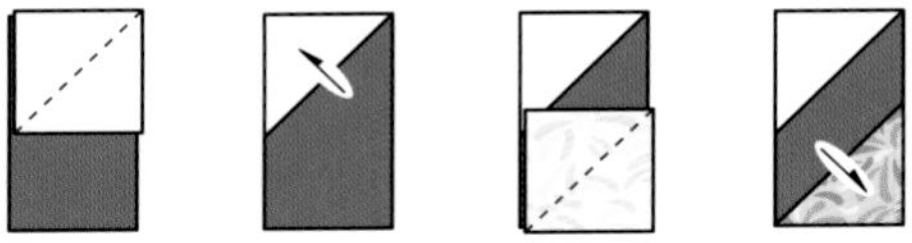

Make 16.

4. Sew the units from steps 2 and 3 together as shown. Press the seams as indicated by the arrows. Make eight of each combination.

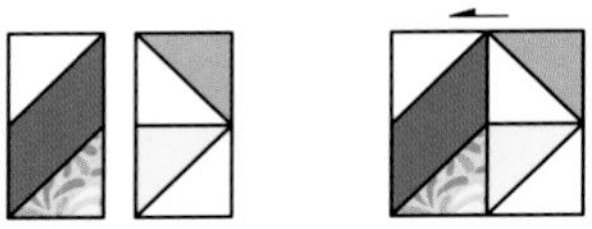

Make 8.

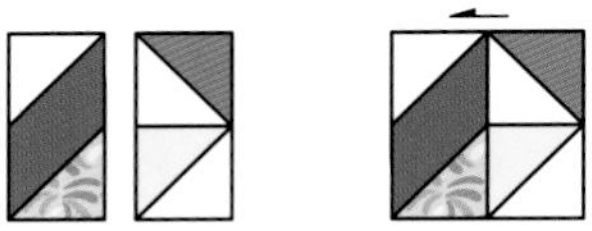

Make 8.

24   *The Blocks*

5. Assemble the units from step 4 as shown.

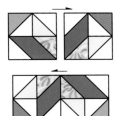
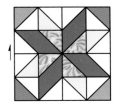

Make 4.

6. Assemble the block using the four units from step 5.

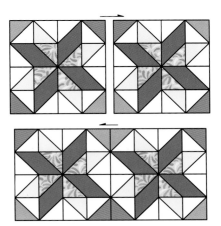

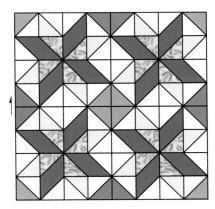

Snow Crystals

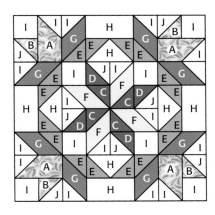

Fabric	Piece	Number and Size to Cut
Main print	A	4 rectangles, 2" x 3½"
	B	2 squares, 2⅜" x 2⅜"
Dark	C	4 squares, 2" x 2"
	D	2 squares, 2⅜" x 2⅜"
Medium	E	16 squares, 2" x 2"
Light	F	4 rectangles, 2" x 3½"
Strong accent	G	8 rectangles, 2" x 3½"
Background	H	8 rectangles, 2" x 3½"
	I	24 squares, 2" x 2"
	J	4 squares, 2⅜" x 2⅜"

Piecing

1. Using the "Folded-Corners Technique" (page 7), place the 2" background squares on the corner of the 2" x 3½" strong-accent rectangles. Sew and trim. Make four in each direction. Press the seams as indicated by the arrows. Repeat with the 2" medium squares on the opposite end, keeping the angles the same.

Make 4.

Make 4.

2. Using the same folded-corners technique, sew 2" background squares on the 2" x 3½" light rectangles. Sew 2" dark squares on the opposite end, keeping the angle the same. Trim and press. Make four.

Make 4.

3. Use the same technique to sew the 2" background squares on one end of the 2" x 3½" main print rectangles. Trim and press. Make four.

Make 4.

4. Place the 2⅜" main-print squares right sides together with two of the 2⅜" background squares. Use the "Layered-Squares Technique" (page 7) to make four triangle-square units. Press the seams toward the main print and trim off any dog-ears. Repeat with the 2⅜" dark and 2⅜" background squares to make four.

Make 4.   Make 4.

5. Sew the triangle-square units from step 4 to the 2" background squares. Press toward the background squares. Make four of each combination.

Make 4 of each.

6. Sew the units from step 3 to the main-print/background units from step 5, as shown. Press the seams toward the triangle-square unit.

Make 4.

7. Sew the units from step 2 to the dark/background units from step 5 as shown. Press. Make four.

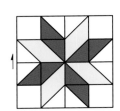

Make 4.

8. Assemble the center star as shown. Press.

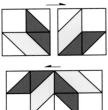

9. Using the folded-corners technique, place a 2" medium square on one corner of each of four 2" x 3½" background rectangles. Stitch, trim, and press toward the medium triangle. Repeat with the opposite corner, stitching the angle in the opposite direction. Make four.

Make 4.

10. Sew the units from step 9 to the remaining 2" x 3½" background rectangles. Press.

Make 4.

11. Sew the units from step 1 to the sides of the unit from step 10. Press toward the center unit. Make four.

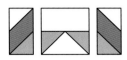

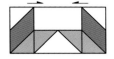

Make 4.

12. Assemble the block as shown, pressing as indicated.

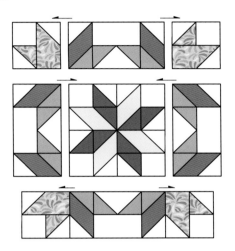

Star of Magi

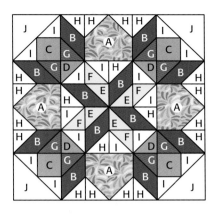

Fabric	Piece	Number and Size to Cut
Main print	A	4 squares, 3½" x 3½"
Dark	B	12 rectangles, 2" x 3½"
Medium	C	4 squares, 2" x 2"
	D	2 squares, 2⅜" x 2⅜"
Light	E	4 squares, 2" x 2"
	F	2 squares, 2⅜" x 2⅜"
Strong accent	G	8 squares, 2" x 2"
Background	H	20 squares, 2" x 2"
	I	8 squares, 2⅜" x 2⅜"; cut 4 once diagonally
	J	2 squares, 3⅞" x 3⅞"; cut once diagonally

Piecing

1. Using the "Folded-Corners Technique" (page 7), place a 2" background square on a 2" x 3½" dark rectangle. Sew along the diagonal. Make four units in one direction and eight units in the opposite direction. Press the seams toward the dark fabric.

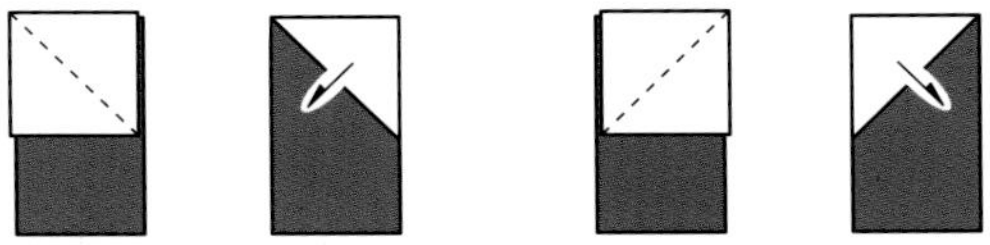

Make 4.   Make 8.

2. On eight units from step 1 (four of one direction and four of the other direction), add a 2" strong-accent square to the other end, making sure that the angles are the same on each piece. Trim and press the seams toward the strong-accent fabric.

Make 4.   Make 4.

3. On the remaining four units from step 1, sew the 2" light squares as shown. Press the seams toward the light fabric. Make four.

Make 4.

4. Sew a 2" background square to the corner of a 3½" main-print square. Repeat as shown for the other corner. Press the seams toward the background and trim the excess to ¼". Make four.

Make 4.

5. Sew one of each of the units from step 2 to each side of the main-print unit from step 4. Press as indicated. Make four.

   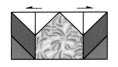

Make 4.

6. Place the 2⅜" medium squares right sides together with two of the 2⅜" background squares. Use the "Layered-Squares Technique" (page 7) to make triangle squares. Repeat with the 2⅜" light and 2⅜" background squares. Press the seams toward the darker fabrics.

Make 4.   Make 4.

7. Sew the triangle squares together as shown. Then sew these units to the units from step 3. Press.

Make 4.   Make 4.

8. Assemble the center section of the block as shown. Press.

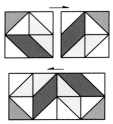 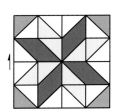

9. Sew the 2⅜" background triangles to the sides of the 2" medium squares as shown. Press toward the triangles. Sew the 3⅞" background triangles to the bias edge of the square-triangle units just made. Make four of these corner units.

Make 4.

28   *The Blocks*

10. Assemble the block as shown. Press.

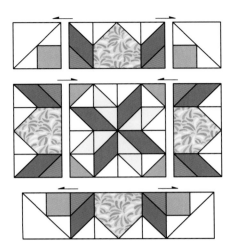

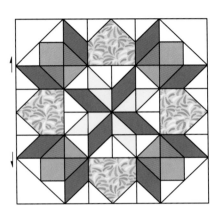

Union Square

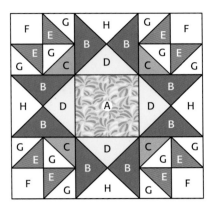

Fabric	Piece	Number and Size to Cut
Main print	A	1 square, 4½" x 4½"
Dark	B	2 squares, 5¼" x 5¼"
Medium	C	2 squares, 2⅞" x 2⅞"
Light	D	1 square, 5¼" x 5¼"
Strong accent	E	4 squares, 2⅞" x 2⅞"
Background	F	4 squares, 2½" x 2½"
	G	6 squares, 2⅞" x 2⅞"
	H	1 square, 5¼" x 5¼"

Piecing

1. Place the 2⅞" medium squares right sides together with two of the 2⅞" background squares. Use the "Layered-Squares Technique" (page 7) to make four triangle squares. Press the seams toward the medium fabric. Repeat with the 2⅞" strong-accent and 2⅞" background squares. Make eight.

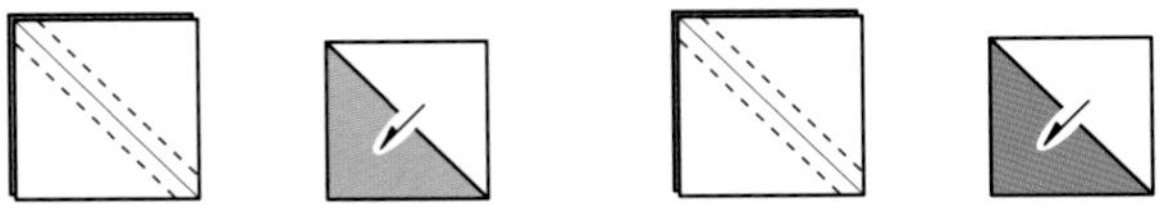

Make 4.

Make 8.

2. Using the 2½" background squares and the tri-angle squares from step 1, assemble the block corner units. Press the seams as indicated by the arrows. Make four.

Make 4.

3. Place a 5¼" dark square right sides together with the 5¼" background square. Use the layered-squares technique to make two triangle squares. Press the seams toward the dark fabric. Repeat with the 5¼" dark and light squares, drawing the diagonal line on the light fabric.

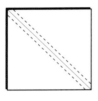

Make 2.

Make 2.

4. Place a dark/background and a dark/light triangle-square unit from step 3 right sides together so the darks are opposite. Draw a line diagonally and sew with a ¼" seam allowance on both sides of the line. Cut the squares apart on the line and press. Make four quarter squares.

Drawn line

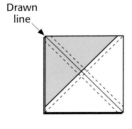

Make 4.

5. Assemble the block as shown, using the 4½" main-print square in the center. Press the seams as indicated by the arrows.

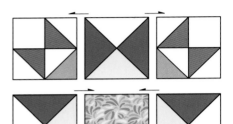

Whirlwind

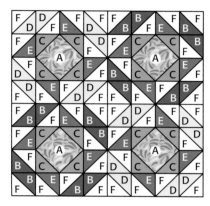

Fabric	Piece	Number and Size to Cut
Main print	A	4 squares, 3½" x 3½"
Dark	B	8 squares, 2⅜" x 2⅜"
Medium	C	16 squares, 2" x 2"
Light	D	8 squares, 2⅜" x 2⅜"
Strong accent	E	8 squares, 2⅜" x 2⅜"
Background	F	24 squares, 2⅜" x 2⅜"

Piecing

1. Using the "Layered-Squares Technique" (page 7), place the 2⅜" background squares right sides together with the dark, strong-accent, and light squares. Draw the diagonal line on the background squares. Sew with a ¼" seam allowance on both sides of the line. Cut the squares apart on the line and press the seams toward the darker fabric. Make 16 of each combination.

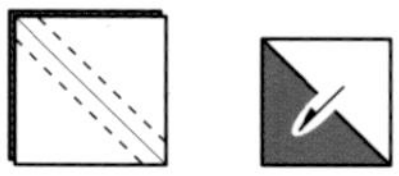

Make 16. 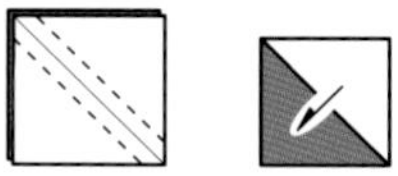   Make 16.

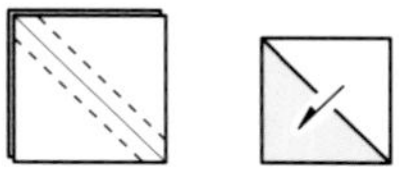

Make 16.

2. Sew the light and strong-accent triangle squares from step 1 together as shown. Repeat with the dark and strong-accent triangle squares. Press the seams as indicated by the arrows. Make eight of each combination.

Make 8.   Make 8.

3. Sew the 2" medium squares to opposite corners of the 3½" main-print squares, using the "Folded-Corners Technique" (page 7). Repeat with the remaining two corners. Make four.

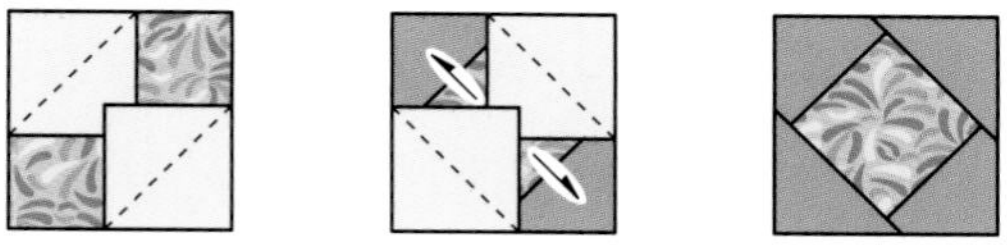

Make 4.

4. Sew the light/strong accent units from step 2 and the units from step 3 together with four light triangle squares from step 1, as shown. Press the seams as indicated by the arrows. Make two units.

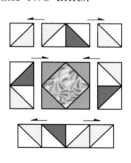 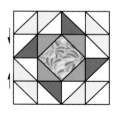

Make 2.

5. Repeat step 4, using the remaining units from steps 2 and 3 and the dark triangle squares from step 1. Press. Make two units.

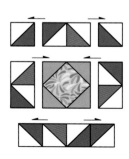 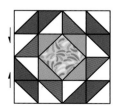

Make 2.

6. Assemble the block as shown, using the units from steps 4 and 5. Press.

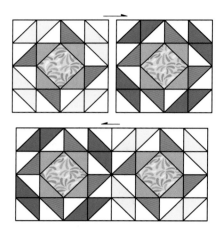

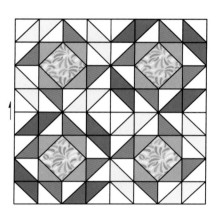

Wyoming Valley Star

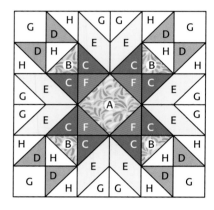

Fabric		Piece	Number and Size to Cut
🪡	Main print	A	1 square, 4½" x 4½"
		B	2 squares, 2⅞" x 2⅞"
⬛	Dark	C	8 squares, 2½" x 2½"
🟦	Medium	D	4 squares, 2⅞" x 2⅞"
☐	Light	E	8 rectangles, 2½" x 4½"
🟥	Strong accent	F	4 squares, 2½" x 2½"
☐	Background	G	12 squares, 2½" x 2½"
		H	6 squares, 2⅞" x 2⅞"

Piecing

1. Using the "Folded-Corners Technique" (page 7), place a 2½" background square on one end of a 2½" x 4½" light rectangle. Sew from corner to corner. Add a 2½" dark square on the opposite end of the light/background unit, making sure that the angle is the same on each

piece. Make four in each direction. Press as indicated by the arrows.

Make 4.

Make 4.

2. Sew the two units together as shown. Press. Make four.

Make 4.

3. Using the "Layered-Squares Technique" (page 7), place the 2⅞" medium squares right sides together with four of the 2⅞" background squares. Draw a diagonal line, stitch, cut, and press. Make eight triangle squares. Repeat, using the 2⅞" main-print squares right sides together with the 2⅞" background squares. Make four triangle squares.

Make 8.   Make 4.

4. Using the 2½" background squares and the triangle squares from step 3, assemble the block corner units as shown. Press. Make four.

Make 4.

5. Using the "Folded-Corners Technique" (page 7), sew the 2½" strong-accent squares to the corners of the 4½" main-print square. Sew opposite corners first, then repeat with the other corners. Trim and press each seam toward the strong-accent fabric.

6. Assemble the block as shown. Press.

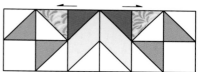

Cutting Chart for Blocks

I have provided this cutting chart of all the blocks for those who like to cut everything at once before sewing. Many of my students prefer to work this way. Choose the blocks you want to make and highlight them on the chart. I suggest that you label a plastic zipper bag for each block and keep the pieces together.

First, cut all the pieces from the main print for the chosen blocks. Begin cutting with the largest piece and then work down the chart, cutting the main-print pieces for each block and placing the pieces in the corresponding plastic bag. Then go to the dark fabric and do the same. Continue with the other fabrics. This way you will have all the pieces for a block in a small bag, and whenever you have time you can sit down and sew a block. Students in my classes have told me how much this helps them.

BLOCK	FABRIC AND CUTTING					
	Main Print	*Dark*	*Medium*	*Light*	*Strong Accent*	*Background*
Arrow Crown	1 square, 3½"	2 squares, 4¼" 4 squares, 2" 4 squares, 2⅜"	8 squares, 2"	4 squares, 2" 8 squares, 2⅜"	4 rectangles, 2" x 3½"	2 squares, 4¼" 12 squares, 2" 4 squares, 2⅜"
Aurora	2 squares, 4¼" 2 squares, 3" ◫	2 squares, 3⅞" ◫	4 squares, 2⅝"	2 squares, 4¼"	1 square, 3½"	4 squares, 3½" 2 squares, 4¼" ⊠
Carpenter's Wheel	8 rectangles, 2" x 3½" 4 squares, 2" 2 squares, 2⅜"	8 rectangles, 2" x 3½"	4 squares, 2"	12 squares, 2"	4 rectangles, 2" x 3½"	40 squares, 2" 2 squares, 2⅜"
Diamond Star	1 square, 3½"	8 rectangles, 2" x 3½" 4 squares, 2" 2 squares, 2⅜"	4 rectangles, 2" x 3½"	8 rectangles, 2" x 3½" 4 squares, 2" 2 squares, 2⅜"	16 squares, 2"	4 squares, 3½" 16 squares, 2"

◫ Cut squares once diagonally.   ⊠ Cut squares twice diagonally.

BLOCK	Main Print	Dark	Medium	Light	Strong Accent	Background
FABRIC AND CUTTING						
Dutch Rose	8 rectangles, 2" x 3½" 4 squares, 2"	8 rectangles, 2" x 3½"	4 squares, 2" 2 squares, 2⅜"	4 rectangles, 2" x 3½"	4 squares, 2"	4 rectangles, 2" x 3½" 32 squares, 2" 2 squares, 2⅜"
Land of the Midnight Sun	1 square, 4½"	4 squares, 4⅞" ◺	4 squares, 2½"	4 squares, 2½"	1 square, 5¼" ⊠	2 squares, 4⅞" ◺ 1 square, 5¼" ⊠ 4 squares, 2½"
Martha's Star	2 squares, 3⅞" ◺	4 squares, 3⅞" ◺	2 squares, 3"	4 squares, 2⅜"	4 squares, 2⅜"	2 squares, 3" 8 squares, 2⅜" 8 squares, 2⅜" ◺ 8 squares, 2"
Next-Door Neighbor	16 squares, 2"	8 rectangles, 2" x 3½"	8 squares, 2"	8 rectangles, 2" x 3½"	16 squares, 2"	16 squares, 2" 16 rectangles, 2" x 3½"
Pieced Stars	16 squares, 2"	16 rectangles, 2" x 3½"	4 squares, 2⅜"	8 squares, 2⅜"	4 squares, 2⅜"	16 squares, 2" 16 squares, 2⅜"
Snow Crystals	4 rectangles, 2" x 3½" 2 squares, 2⅜"	4 squares, 2" 2 squares, 2⅜"	16 squares, 2"	4 rectangles, 2" x 3½"	8 rectangles, 2" x 3½"	8 rectangles, 2" x 3½" 24 squares, 2" 4 squares, 2⅜"
Star of Magi	4 squares, 3½"	12 rectangles, 2" x 3½"	4 squares, 2" 2 squares, 2⅜"	4 squares, 2" 2 squares, 2⅜"	8 squares, 2"	20 squares, 2" 4 squares, 2⅜" 4 squares, 2⅜" ◺ 2 squares, 3⅞" ◺
Union Square	1 square, 4½"	2 squares, 5¼"	2 squares, 2⅞"	1 square, 5¼"	4 squares, 2⅞"	4 squares, 2½" 6 squares, 2⅞" 1 square, 5¼"
Whirlwind	4 squares, 3½"	8 squares, 2⅜"	16 squares, 2"	8 squares, 2⅜"	8 squares, 2⅜"	24 squares, 2⅜"
Wyoming Valley Star	1 square, 4½" 2 squares, 2⅞"	8 squares, 2½"	4 squares, 2⅞"	8 rectangles, 2½" x 4½"	4 squares, 2½"	12 squares, 2½" 6 squares, 2⅞"

◺ *Cut squares once diagonally.*   ⊠ *Cut squares twice diagonally.*

Color Variations

Because you'll need four additional blocks for the king-size sampler quilt—18 blocks in all—I've included these cutting instructions for alternate color placements for four of the blocks.

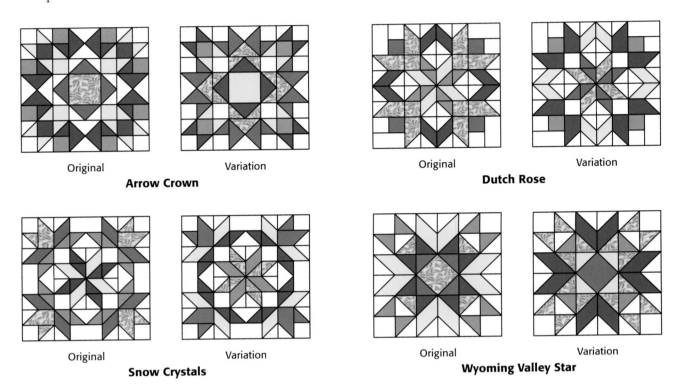

Original   Variation
Arrow Crown

Original   Variation
Dutch Rose

Original   Variation
Snow Crystals

Original   Variation
Wyoming Valley Star

| BLOCK | FABRIC AND CUTTING | | | | | |
	Main Print	Dark	Medium	Light	Strong Accent	Background
Arrow Crown	1 square, 4¼" 8 squares, 2"	4 rectangles, 2" x 3½" 4 squares, 2⅜"	4 squares, 2"	1 square, 3½" 4 squares, 2⅜"	2 squares, 4¼" 4 squares, 2⅜"	1 square, 4¼" 16 squares, 2" 4 squares, 2⅜"
Dutch Rose	4 rectangles, 2" x 3½"	8 rectangles, 2" x 3½"	4 squares, 2"	8 rectangles, 2" x 3½"	4 squares, 2" 2 squares, 2⅜"	4 rectangles, 2" x 3½" 36 squares, 2" 2 squares, 2⅜"
Snow Crystals	4 squares, 2" 2 squares, 2⅜"	16 squares, 2"	4 rectangles, 2" x 3½"	8 rectangles, 2" x 3½"	4 rectangles, 2" x 3½" 2 squares, 2⅜"	8 rectangles, 2" x 3½" 24 squares, 2" 4 squares, 2⅜"
Wyoming Valley Star	4 squares, 2⅞" 8 squares, 2½"	8 rectangles, 2½" x 4½"	2 squares, 2⅞"	4 squares, 2½"	1 square, 4½"	12 squares, 2½" 6 squares, 2⅞"

Lap-Size
Star-Studded Sampler

Finished quilt: 60" x 84" ★ Finished block: 12"

Have fun choosing the eight blocks to make this lap-size sampler. Keep in mind when making this sampler that two of the blocks will be set square with the setting triangles, and six blocks will be set on point using the framing strips.

Materials

Yardage is based on 42"-wide fabric.

2½ yards of main print for blocks and outer border

1⅜ yards of dark print for setting triangles

1¼ yards of background fabric for blocks

1 yard of medium print for block frames

¾ yard of light print for inner border

⅝ yard of dark for blocks

⅝ yard of medium for blocks

⅝ yard of light for blocks

⅝ yard of strong accent for blocks

5 yards of fabric for backing

¾ yard of fabric for binding

66" x 90" piece of batting

Cutting

Before cutting the blocks, cut the border strips from the main print.

From the lengthwise grain of the main print, cut:

★ 2 strips, 6½" x 72½"*

★ 2 strips, 6½" x 60½"*

From the dark-print setting fabric, cut:

★ 4 squares, 9⅜" x 9⅜", cut diagonally once to make 8 triangles

★ 2 squares, 20¼" x 20¼", cut diagonally twice to make 8 triangles

★ 2 squares, 7⅞" x 7⅞", cut diagonally once to make 4 triangles

From the block-frame fabric, cut:

★ 1 strip, 17½" x 42", crosscut into 12 pieces, 3" x 17½"

★ 1 strip, 12½" x 42", crosscut into 12 pieces, 3" x 12½"

From the inner-border fabric, cut:

★ 7 strips, 3" x 42", crosscut into 6 pieces, 3" x 25½"; 4 pieces, 3" x 13½"; and 4 pieces, 3" x 10½"

From the binding fabric, cut:

★ 8 strips, 2½" x 42"

* These are the exact measurements, but you may want to cut the border strips an inch or two longer. Then measure your quilt top through the center and cut them to the exact length later.

Piecing

1. Make eight blocks following the block cutting and piecing directions.

2. **Straight-set blocks with setting triangles.** Sew the 9⅜" dark-print triangles to opposite sides of the two blocks chosen for the straight set. Press the seams toward the triangles. Sew the remaining triangles to the other sides.

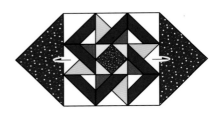

Make 2.

Teacher's Tip
When sewing triangles to squares, sew with the bias edge on the bottom whenever possible.

3. **On-point blocks with frames.** Sew the 3" x 12½" framing pieces to opposite sides of the six blocks to be set on point. Press the seams toward the framing strips. Sew the 3" x 17½" pieces to the remaining sides of the blocks. Press.

Make 6.

4. **Inner border.** Center a 3" x 25½" inner-border piece on the long side of a 20¼" dark-print setting triangle. Stitch and press toward the inner border. Using a ruler with a 45° angle, place the 45° line on the seam, and line up the

edge of the ruler with the triangle edge; trim away the excess inner-border strip. Make six.

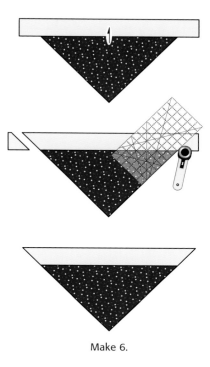

Make 6.

5. **Corners.** Sew a 3" x 10½" inner-border piece to the side of a 7⅞" dark-print setting triangle. Press the seams toward the inner border. Sew a 3" x 13½" inner-border piece to the other side of the triangle. Press. Place a ruler along the edge of the triangle and trim away the excess fabric so the triangle edge is even. Make four.

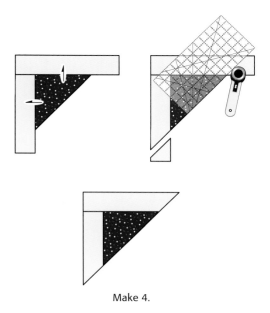

Make 4.

6. Assemble the quilt top in diagonal rows as shown.

7. **Outer borders.** Fold a 6½" x 72½" main-print border in half to find the center of the strip; pin the center of the strip to the center of one side of the quilt top; then pin the ends to the edge of the quilt top. Sew the border onto the quilt, using a ¼" seam allowance. Repeat with the other side border. Press toward the outer border. Fold the 6½" x 60½" main-print border strips in half to find the center. Pin the centers of the border strips to the centers of the top and bottom of the quilt; sew, using a ¼" seam allowance. Press.

Finishing

1. Layer the quilt top with the backing and batting, and baste the layers together.

2. Quilt as desired. The quilt shown was quilted by machine. The block backgrounds and the border were stippled. There are curving lines in the large triangular areas to give the look of fireworks.

3. Using the 2½" binding strips, make and attach the binding, referring to "Binding" (page 8).

4. Label your quilt.

Queen-Size
Star-Studded Sampler

Finished quilt: 86" x 86" ★ Finished block: 12"

Choose 13 blocks for this queen-size sampler. Four blocks are set square with setting triangles, and nine blocks are set on point with framing strips.

Materials

Yardage is based on 42"-wide fabric.

3 yards of main print for blocks and outer border

2 yards of background fabric for blocks

1⅝ yards of light print for setting triangles

1½ yards of dark print for block frames

1 yard of dark for blocks

1 yard of medium for blocks

1 yard of light for blocks

1 yard of strong accent for blocks

⅞ yard of dark print for inner border

¾ yard of fabric for binding

7½ yards of fabric for backing

90" x 90" square of batting

Cutting

Before cutting the blocks, cut the border strips from the main print.

From the lengthwise grain of the main print, cut:

★ 2 strips, 7½" x 72½"*

★ 2 strips, 7½" x 86½"*

From the light print for setting triangles, cut:

★ 8 squares, 9⅜" x 9⅜", cut diagonally once to make 16 triangles

★ 2 squares, 20¼" x 20¼", cut diagonally twice to make 8 triangles

★ 2 squares, 7⅞" x 7⅞", cut diagonally once to make 4 triangles

From the block-frame fabric, cut:

★ 18 pieces, 3" x 12½"

★ 18 pieces, 3" x 17½"

From the inner-border fabric, cut:

★ 8 strips, 3" x 42", crosscut into 8 pieces, 3" x 25½"; 4 pieces, 3" x 13½"; and 4 pieces, 3" x 10½"

From the binding fabric, cut:

★ 9 strips, 2½" x 42"

* *These are the exact measurements, but you may want to cut the border strips an inch or two longer. Then measure your quilt top through the center and cut them to the exact length later.*

Piecing

1. Make 13 blocks following the block cutting and piecing directions.

2. **Straight-set blocks with setting triangles.** Sew the 9⅜" setting triangles to opposite sides of the blocks chosen for the straight set. Press the seams toward the triangles. Sew triangles to the remaining sides. Make four.

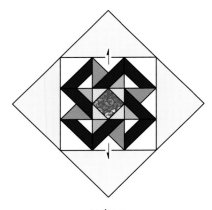

Make 4.

3. **On-point blocks with frames.** Sew the 3" x 12½" framing pieces to opposite sides of the blocks to be set on point. Press the seams toward the framing strips. Sew the 3" x 17½" pieces to the remaining sides of the blocks. Make nine.

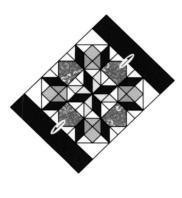

Make 9.

4. **Inner border.** Center a 3" x 25½" inner-border piece on the long side of a 20¼" setting triangle; pin and sew. Press toward the inner border. Using a ruler with a 45° angle, place the 45° line on the seam and line up the edge of the ruler with the triangle edge; trim away

the excess fabric of the inner-border strip. Make eight.

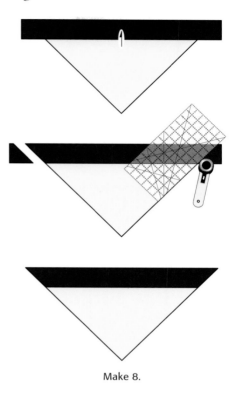

Make 8.

5. **Corners.** Sew a 3" x 10½" inner-border piece to the side of a 7⅞" setting triangle. Press the seam toward the border piece. Sew a 3" x 13½" inner-border piece to the other side of the triangle. Press. Place a ruler along the edge of the triangle and trim away the excess fabric so the triangle edge is even. Make four.

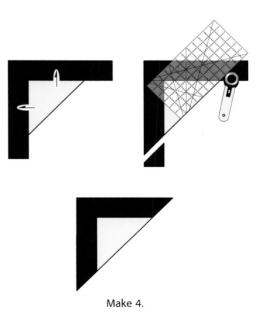

Make 4.

6. Assemble the quilt top in diagonal rows as shown.

7. **Outer borders.** Fold a 7½" x 72½" main-print border in half to find the center of the strip; pin the center of the strip to the center of one side of the quilt top; then pin the ends to the edge of the quilt top. Sew the border onto the quilt, using a ¼" seam allowance. Repeat with the other side border. Press toward the outer border. Fold the 7½" x 86½" main-print border strips in half to find the center. Pin the centers of the border strips to the centers of the top and bottom; sew, using a ¼" seam allowance. Press.

Finishing

1. Layer the quilt top with the backing and batting, and baste.

2. Quilt as desired. The quilt shown was quilted by machine, with stippling in the block backgrounds and a commercial quilting design in the large triangular areas. There are straight lines in the inner border; the outer border is stipple quilted.

3. Using the 2½" binding strips, make and attach binding, referring to "Binding" (page 8).

4. Label your quilt.

King-Size
Star-Studded Sampler

Finished quilt: 88" x 112" ★ **Finished block: 12"**

You will need 18 blocks for the king-size sampler (you will have to repeat 4 blocks). When you repeat a block, vary the fabric placement. Refer to "Color Variations" (page 36), where I've included a cutting chart for the alternate color placements in the 4 blocks that I used in this sampler.

Choose 6 blocks that will be set square with setting triangles and 12 blocks that will be set on point using the framing strips.

Materials

Yardage is based on 42"-wide fabric.

3⅝ yards of main print for blocks and outer border

2¾ yards of background fabric for blocks

2¼ yards of fabric for setting triangles

2 yards of fabric for block frames

1½ yards of dark for blocks

1½ yards of medium for blocks

1½ yards of light for blocks

1 yard of strong accent for blocks

1 yard of fabric for inner border

8 yards of fabric for backing

1 yard of fabric for binding

96" x 120" piece of batting

Cutting

Before cutting the blocks, cut the border strips from the main print.

From the lengthwise grain of the main print, cut:

★ 2 strips, 8½" x 96½"*

★ 2 strips, 8½" x 88½"*

From the setting-triangle fabric, cut:

★ 12 squares, 9⅜" x 9⅜", cut diagonally once for 24 triangles

★ 3 squares, 20¼" x 20¼", cut diagonally twice for 10 triangles (2 extra)

★ 2 squares, 7⅞" x 7⅞", cut diagonally once for 4 triangles

From the block-frame fabric, cut:

★ 24 pieces, 3" x 17½"

★ 24 pieces, 3" x 12½"

From the inner-border fabric, cut:

★ 10 pieces, 3" x 25½"

★ 4 pieces, 3" x 13½"

★ 4 pieces, 3" x 10½"

From the binding fabric, cut

★ 11 strips, 2½" x 42"

* These are the exact measurements, but you may want to cut the border strips an inch or two longer. Then measure your quilt top through the center and cut them to the exact length later.

Piecing

1. Make 18 blocks following the block cutting and piecing directions.

2. **Straight-set blocks with setting triangles.** Sew 9⅜" setting triangles to opposite sides of the six blocks chosen for the straight set. Press the seams toward the triangles. Sew the other triangles to the remaining two sides, and press.

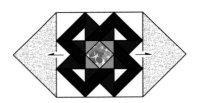

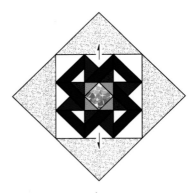

Make 6.

3. **On-point blocks with frames.** Sew the 3" x 12½" framing pieces to opposite sides of the 12 blocks to be set on point. Press the seams toward the framing strips. Add the 3" x 17½" pieces to the remaining sides of the blocks. Press.

Make 12.

4. **Inner border.** Center a 3" x 25½" inner-border piece on the long side of a 20¼" setting triangle. Stitch and press toward the inner border. Using a ruler with a 45° angle, place the 45° line on the seam and line up the edge of the ruler with the triangle edge; trim away the excess fabric of the inner-border strip. Make 10.

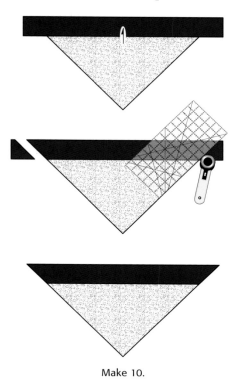

Make 10.

5. **Corners.** Sew a 3" x 10½" inner-border piece to the side of a 7⅞" setting triangle. Press the seam toward the inner border. Sew a 3" x 13½" inner-border piece to the other side of the triangle. Press. Place a ruler along the edge of the triangle and trim away the excess fabric so the triangle edge is even. Make four.

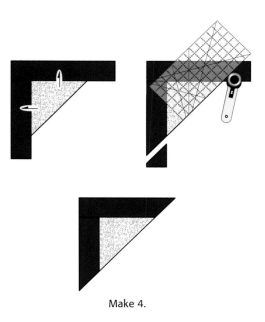

Make 4.

6. Assemble the quilt top in diagonal rows as shown in the diagram.

7. **Outer borders.** Fold the 8½" x 96½" main-print border strips in half to find the center of the strips. Match and pin the center of one strip to the center of one side of the quilt; pin at the ends and in between. Sew the border onto the quilt, using a ¼" seam allowance. Repeat for the other side border. Press toward the outer border. Repeat for the 8½" x 88½" main-print border strips, sewing them to the top and bottom of the quilt. Press.

Finishing

1. Layer the quilt top with the backing and batting, and baste.

2. Quilt as desired. The quilt shown was machine quilted, with stippling in the block backgrounds and outer border, and a feathered design in the large triangular areas and the block frames. There are straight lines in the inner border.

3. Using the 2½" binding strips, make and attach binding, referring to "Binding" (page 8).

4. Label your quilt.

Sweet Pea Sampler

Finished quilt: 64½" x 77" ★ Finished block: 12"

Choose 12 blocks to make this charming blue, yellow, and white sampler with a pieced border. Or vary the colors, using your favorites. Notice how the light print used for the sashing between the blocks is also used as an inner border—this makes the blocks appear to float inside the outer borders.

Materials

Yardage is based on 42"-wide fabric.

2½ yards of background fabric for blocks and pieced border

2⅛ yards of dark print for inner and outer borders and binding

1½ yards of main print for blocks, cornerstones, and border

1¼ yards of light print for sashing and inner border

⅞ yard of light for blocks

¾ yard of dark for blocks

¾ yard of medium for blocks

¾ yard of strong accent for blocks

¼ yard *each* of two accent prints for border (accent 1 and accent 2)

4 yards of fabric for backing

70" x 82" piece of batting

Cutting

From the light print for sashing and inner border, cut:

★ 6 strips, 2½" x 42", crosscut into 17 rectangles, 2½" x 12½"

★ 3 strips, 2⅞" x 42"

★ 4 strips, 3½" x 42

From the dark print for borders and binding, cut:

★ 15 strips, 3" x 42"

★ 8 strips, 2½" x 42"

From the background, cut:

★ 6 strips, 3½" x 42", crosscut into 56 squares, 3½" x 3½"; cut diagonally twice to make 224 triangles

★ 2 squares, 3¼" x 3¼", cut diagonally once to make 4 triangles

From *each* of the accent 1 and accent 2, cut:

★ 3 strips, 2" x 42", crosscut into 58 squares, 2" x 2"

From the main print, cut:

★ 6 squares, 2½" x 2½"

★ 6 strips, 3½" x 42", crosscut into 58 squares, 3½" x 3½"

Piecing the Quilt Center

1. Piece 12 blocks following the block cutting and piecing directions. Be sure that your blocks measure 12½" square and that you sew with an exact ¼" seam allowance. The inner portion of your quilt top needs to be accurate so that the pieced borders will fit properly.

2. Referring to the quilt diagram on page 53, sew the top together in four rows of three blocks each, using the 2½" x 12½" light-print sashing strips between the blocks. Piece three sashing rows, using the 2½" main-print cornerstones between 2½" x 12½" sashing pieces. Press all seams toward the light-print sashing strips.

3. Sew two 3½" x 42" light-print inner-border strips together with a diagonal seam. Press the seam open. Make two. Cut each strip to 54½". Sew these strips to the sides of the pieced top.

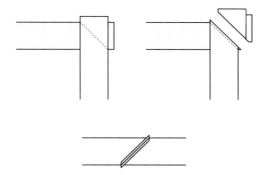

4. Cut one of the 2⅞" x 42" inner-border strips in half. Sew one long strip and one short strip together with a diagonal seam. Press the seam open. Make two. Cut each strip to 46½". Sew these strips to the top and bottom of the pieced top. Press the seams toward the inner-border strip.

5. Sew two 3" x 42" dark-print border strips together with a diagonal seam. Make two. Cut each strip to 59¼". Sew these strips to the sides of the pieced top. Press the seams toward the dark-print border.

6. Cut one of the 3" x 42" dark-print border strips in half. Sew one long strip and one short strip together with a diagonal seam. Press the seam open. Make two. Cut each strip to 51½". Sew the strips to the top and bottom of the pieced top. Press the seams toward the dark-print border.

Piecing the Border

1. Sew the 3½" background triangles to the sides of the 2" accent 1 squares as shown. Press the seams toward the triangles. Repeat with the 2" accent 2 squares. Make 54 of each. Note that the background triangles were cut slightly oversized. You will trim the border units later if needed.

Make 54.   Make 54.

2. For the end pieces, sew a 3½" background triangle to one side of an accent square as shown. Sew a background triangle to the opposite side of another accent square. Make two of each accent color in each position, as shown.

Make 2.   Make 2.   Make 2.   Make 2.

3. Sew an accent 1 unit from step 1 to the side of a 3½" main-print square as shown. Press the seam allowance toward the accent unit. Repeat with an accent 2 unit on the opposite side of the main-print square. Make 46.

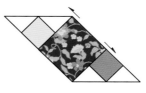

Make 46.

4. Sew four of the accent 1 units from step 1 to the sides of four 3½" main-print squares as shown. Repeat with the accent 2 units. Make four of each combination.

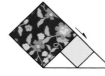 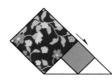

Make 4.   Make 4.

5. Add the units from step 2 to the units from step 4 as shown. Make two of each combination for the end pieces.

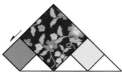 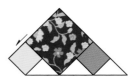

Make 2.   Make 2.

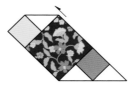 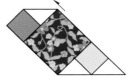

Make 2.   Make 2.

6. Assemble the corner units as shown, using four 3½" main-print squares, accent 1 and accent 2 units from step 1, and the 3¼" background triangles. The corner triangle may be a little large but can be trimmed after it is sewn on. Make two of each combination.

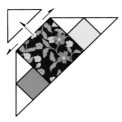

Make 2.

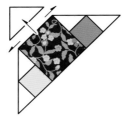

Make 2.

7. Assemble the pieced borders as shown. Press all the seams in one direction. Trim the edges as needed, keeping a ¼" seam allowance beyond the points of the squares.

8. Sew the side borders to the quilt top, starting and stopping ¼" from the ends of the top. The longest side of the border goes next to the dark inner border. Repeat with the top and bottom borders, starting and stopping ¼" from the ends on each border. There should be no gap where the two borders come together. Fold the unit on a 45° angle with right sides of the border pieces together. Sew the two accent squares together and press toward the darker fabric. Press the pieced border seams toward the dark inner border.

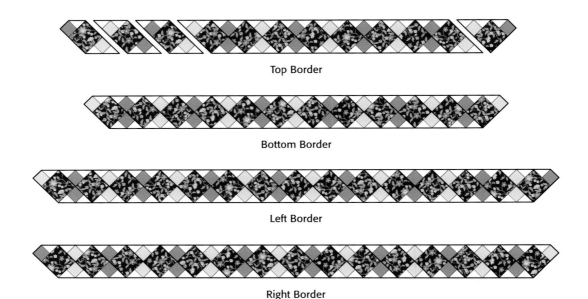

Top Border

Bottom Border

Left Border

Right Border

9. Sew the corner units to the quilt top as shown in the quilt diagram. Make sure to match the accent colors with the ones on the pieced border.

Outer Border

1. Sew two 3" x 42" dark-print border strips together with a diagonal seam. Repeat to make four long strips. Cut two of the strips to 72¾". Sew these strips to the sides of the quilt. Press the seams toward the outer border.

2. Cut the remaining two strips to 65". Sew the strips to the top and bottom of the quilt. Press the seams toward the dark-print outer borders.

Finishing

1. Layer the quilt top, batting, and backing, and baste the layers together.

2. Quilt as desired. The quilt shown was machine quilted in the ditch and the background was stipple quilted. A leaf pattern was quilted in the sashing and framing border strips. The dark-print borders have two lines of straight stitching in each.

3. Using the 2½" binding strips, make and attach the binding, referring to "Binding" (page 8).

4. Label your quilt.

Star Quartet

Finished quilt: 39½" x 39½" ★ Finished block: 12"

Choose four of your favorite blocks to make a dramatic wall hanging. The light-print sashing fabric is also used for an inner border, which makes the blocks appear to float. A darker fabric will make them appear framed and more like four individual blocks. If you want that look, you may want to choose a lighter fabric for the second border next to it. For this wall hanging I used Star of Magi (page 27), Carpenter's Wheel (page 14), Snow Crystals (page 25), and Dutch Rose (page 17). All of these blocks have the same center star, which is also used in the corners of the border.

Materials

Yardage is based on 42"-wide fabric.

1⅛ yards of dark print for borders 2 and 4 and binding

1 yard of main print for blocks and border 3

¾ yard of background fabric for blocks

½ yard of dark for blocks (red)

½ yard of light for blocks (peach)

½ yard of medium for blocks (green)

⅜ yard of light print for sashing and border 1

¼ yard of strong accent for blocks (gold)

2½ yards of fabric for backing*

45" x 45" square of batting

If your fabric is at least 42" wide after prewashing, 1¼ yards will be enough.

Cutting

From the light print for sashing and border 1, cut:

★ 4 rectangles, 2" x 12½"

★ 2 strips, 1½" x 26"

★ 2 strips, 1½" x 28"

From the main print, cut:

★ 4 strips, 3½" x 42"

★ 9 squares, 2" x 2"

★ 4 squares, 2⅜" x 2⅜"

From the light, cut:

★ 16 squares, 2" x 2"

★ 8 squares, 2⅜" x 2⅜"

From the dark, cut:

★ 16 rectangles, 2" x 3½"

From the dark print for borders and binding, cut:

★ 8 strips, 2" x 42"

★ 24 squares, 2" x 2"

★ 4 squares, 2⅜" x 2⅜"

★ 5 strips, 2½" x 42"

Piecing

1. Make four blocks following the block cutting and piecing directions.

2. Arrange and sew the blocks together using the 2" sashing strips and a 2" main-print square as shown. Press as indicated by the arrows.

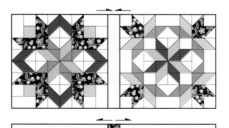
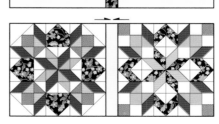

3. Sew the 1½" x 26" border 1 strips to the sides of the quilt top, then sew the 1½" x 28" strips to the top and bottom. Press toward the borders.

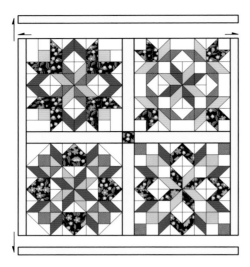

 Teacher's Tip
Pin the border strips to the quilt top at each end. If one piece is slightly longer, sew with the longer piece on the bottom. The feed dogs will help ease in any excess fabric.

Making the Pieced Border

1. Using the "Folded-Corners Technique" (page 7), sew the 2" light squares to the 2" x 3½" dark rectangles as shown. Trim the seams to ¼" and press the seams toward the light. Make 16.

Make 16.

2. On eight units from step 1, sew the 2" dark-print squares to the opposite end; the angle should match the triangle on the other end. Trim and press toward the dark-print triangles.

Repeat to sew the 2" main-print squares on the opposite end of the remaining units from step 1. Make sure the angle is the same. Trim and press.

Make 8.   Make 8.

3. Place four 2⅜" light squares right sides together with the four 2⅜" dark-print squares. Use the "Layered-Squares Technique" (page 7) to make eight triangle squares. Press. Repeat with the 2⅜" light and 2⅜" main-print squares.

Make 8.   Make 8.

4. Sew the triangle-square units from step 3 to the 2" dark-print squares as shown. Press.

Make 8.   Make 8.

5. Sew the units together as shown.

Make 4.   Make 4.   Make 4.   Make 4.

6. Assemble the corner star blocks as shown. Press as indicated by the arrows. Make four.

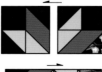 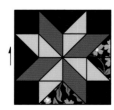

Make 4.

7. Sew 2" dark-print border strips to opposite sides of a 3½" main-print strip. Press toward the dark-print strips. Make four.

Make 4.

8. Measure the quilt through the center and cut the border units to this measurement. Assemble the quilt top as shown.

Finishing

1. Layer the quilt top, batting, and backing, and baste the layers together.

2. Quilt as desired. The quilt shown was machine quilted in the ditch, and the main-print border was stipple-quilted.

3. Using the 2½" binding strips, make and attach the binding, referring to "Binding" (page 8).

4. Add a hanging sleeve, if desired, and label your quilt.

Trio of Stars
Table Runner

Finished quilt: 18" x 45" ★ Finished block: 12"

Table runners are wonderful projects for practicing all your skills, from choosing colors and fabrics and piecing, to experimenting with various quilting techniques. Have fun experimenting, and then you'll have a new decorating accessory to sweeten the deal!

Materials

Yardage is based on 42"-wide fabric.

⅞ yard of main print for blocks, border, and binding

½ yard of background fabric for blocks

⅜ yard of dark for blocks

⅜ yard of medium for blocks

⅜ yard of light for blocks

⅜ yard of strong accent for blocks

1½ yards of fabric for backing

23" x 50" piece of batting

Cutting

From the main print, cut:

★ 1 strip, 2" x 42", crosscut into 2 rectangles, 2" x 12½"

★ 3 strips, 3½" x 42"; cut 2 strips to 3½" x 39½" and 1 strip into 2 rectangles, 3½" x 18½"

★ 4 strips, 2½" x 42"

Piecing

1. Make any three blocks for the table runner following the block cutting and piecing directions.

2. Sew the 2" x 12½" main-print rectangles between the blocks as shown. Press the seam allowance toward the print fabric.

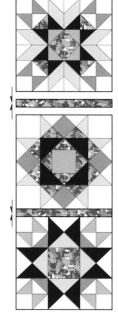

3. Sew the 3½" x 39½" main-print strips to the sides of the blocks. Sew the 3½" x 18½" main-print border rectangles to the ends. Press the seam allowances toward the main print.

Finishing

1. Layer the quilt top, batting, and backing, and baste the layers together.

2. Quilt as desired. The table runner shown was machine quilted in the ditch of the blocks, and stipple-quilted in the border.

3. Using the 2½" binding strips, make and attach the binding, referring to "Binding" (page 8).

4. Label your table runner.

Around the Block Tote Bag

Finished bag: 18" x 18" ★ Finished block: 12"